M000199433

Making Sense of
Microaggressions

First edition published 2021

Open Voices
www.open-voices.com

© Susan Cousins and Barry Diamond 2021
All rights reserved.

No part of this publication may be
reproduced, stored in a retrieval system,
transmitted, or utilised in any form by any
means, electronic, mechanical,
photocopying or recording or otherwise
without permission in writing from the
publishers.

Making Sense of Microaggressions

ISBN: 9781739955304

A CIP catalogue record for this book is
available from the British Library.

MAKING
SENSE
OF

Dedicated to . . .

Susan >
for my sons, Alex and Tod.

Barry >
for our boys, Oliver and Jack.

MICROaggressIONS

contents

Where did the WORD come from?

Interstate Condensed Ultra Black > Interstate Condensed Regular > ROSELLA DECO

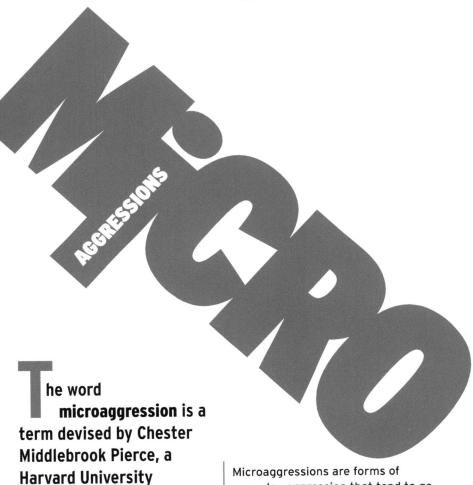

MICRO AGGRESSIONS

The word **microaggression** is a term devised by Chester Middlebrook Pierce, a Harvard University Professor.

He described it as . . .

" SUBTLE, STUNNING AND OFTEN AUTOMATIC NON-VERBAL EXCHANGES WHICH ARE PUT-DOWNS. "

Pierce, Carew, Pierce-Gonzalez, and Willis, 1978, p.66

Microaggressions are forms of everyday oppression that tend to go unseen and unacknowledged.

They contain subtle undertones and hidden messages that are both unintentional and deliberate.

This book aims to uncover what lies beneath these verbal and non-verbal slights that blight the lives of black, brown and people of colour.

One person's banter is another person's put-down.

INTRODUCTION

Interstate Condensed Black > Rockwell Bold > Superclarendon Black

This book is both a graphic and written depiction of what it's like to be at the receiving end of microaggressions and the resulting impact of those encounters.

It is a joint venture between two people hoping to make the invisible visible and to make sense of what, why and how microaggressions are delivered. It feels as if we're at a time and place where we need to understand more about how microaggressions manifest in our daily lives.

Throughout this book we've used examples that have arisen from the experiences of friends, family and colleagues gathered over many years; where conversations about these interactions took place and yet nobody could name.

There's been a gap in our knowledge and understanding of these covert slights that are commonplace and yet hidden and camouflaged in a language that is normalised. They are obvious for all to see and yet so easily deniable and resistant to examination because of the sly workings of a mechanism that hides from open and honest conversation.

Microaggressions can put you down, put you in your place and leave you doubting your sanity. This accessible book attempts to explore these everyday occurrences, these acts of understated trickery, that are cumulatively shattering and forcefully denied in white spaces; where acts of racism are often taken as anything other than racism. Microaggressions are repetitive in nature, occurring in snatches of conversation, and may or may not be consciously present in the minds of others who claim innocence.

We hope this book plants the seeds for change as we move towards a society where racism holds no power and where microaggressions are checked, challenged and erradicated from everyday use.

CAN I touch YOUR HAIR?

Interstate Condensed Black > Rockwell Bold > Superclarendon Black

Hair can also act as a signifier of militancy or anger; a challenge to the norms of society. Our hair story and the meaning we make of it changes with time and has its own history. **You are not obliged to explain the colour, texture and style of your hair** because you wear your hair differently, even if the question is wrapped up in a compliment.

The Impact

A loaded and inappropriate request experienced in everyday life, where hair becomes a marker of oppression and difference, where your hair ceases to belong to you and where others feel entitled to invade your personal space.

Your hair is there as an object to be touched, falling into the grasp of white hands. A stranger running their fingers through your hair is a mean touch felt by many black, brown and people of colour, where hair has become a 'thing' at the disposal of others!

In this interaction you are not being considered with normal courtesy or etiquette because your hair has become something for other people's gratification. No thought or feeling is given to your personal space and there is an intention to violate your boundaries in a physical and overt expression of your difference.

▶ If this occurs when you're a child, you may grow up to feel there is something wrong with your hair, that you're not normal; you may feel ashamed and embarrassed.

▶ As an adult you may feel disrespected and unsure how to respond.

▶ This is a violation of your privacy, and you should be treated with respect.

▶ **You may feel to blame when you are not**, or that you should have taken a stand against the person who did this, but you may not have had the words or the language to challenge this experience.

▶ We are often caught off guard but if it happens again you could say *'may I touch your hair first'* or *'no you can't'*.

04

WHERE

are you from?

I mean, where

ARE YOU

really from?

*No, where are
you originally*

FROM?

Blacksword › **Interstate condensed Ultra Black**

The Impact

This is a challenge to your citizenship where the underlying message is the implication that you don't belong, that you shouldn't have rights and access to this country; that you belong somewhere else even when you don't know where that 'somewhere else' may be.

And you may never have been to a place called 'somewhere else'.

This type of questioning is generally not naïve, and it is not a means of reaching out to get to know you, to build a connection or build a relationship with you.

It is more than likely that the instigator of such questioning is hoping to pocket the knowledge, to shore up their own stereotypes because they feel threatened. They are expressing covert views about immigration and a deep distrust regarding your status as a citizen of this country.

It may be unconscious, it may be conscious, but it is not innocent.

▶ You may find yourself challenged to come up with a rapid-fire response.

▶ You may be caught off guard and unable to find the answer you would love to give. **But it is not your responsibility to be clever and quick-witted all the time and there is no need for you to feel you should have responded with more assertion.** You are living while a person of colour and you are entitled to make choices and decisions that you are comfortable with, even if that means walking away. It's useful to make notes on how you would like to respond if it happens again, and it's useful to practise those responses; so next time you might be less taken by surprise.

▶ Overly questioning anybody about anything is a form of bullying; a communication style that on the surface seems like an innocent inquiry but it is more than likely to be about controlling the conversation and intentionally inflicting discomfort.

▶ It is a form of 'othering' based on a partial understanding of the patterns and reasons for migration to this country.

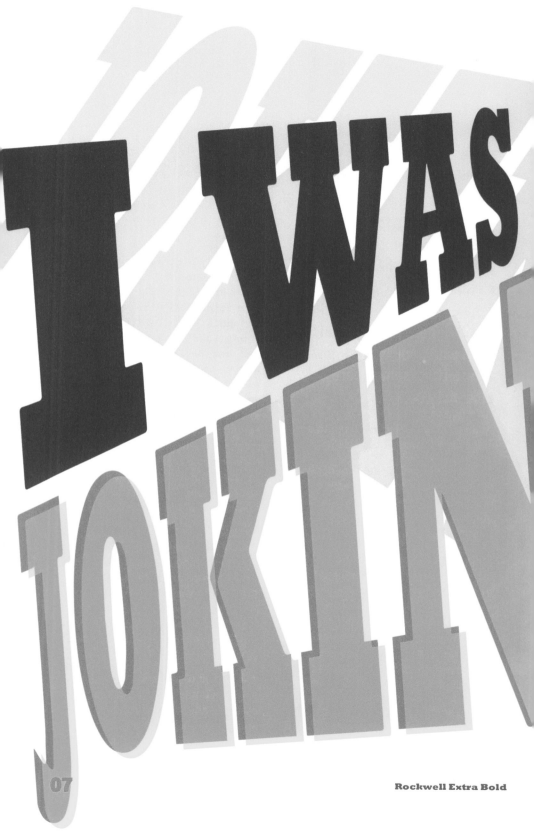

I WAS JOKIN

Rockwell Extra Bold

ONLY

The Impact

Racist jokes, however they are dressed up as humour, are normally only funny to people who share similar viewpoints, because jokes like this aren't funny for black, brown or people of colour and yet they still remain amusing to some white people.

And, given the right conditions of time, place, and concealment away from an audience of colour, white people may let loose their true thoughts and feelings.

If that white person:

> 'found themselves in a room full of black people, and was asked if they cared to repeat the "joke" again, funnily enough they wouldn't feel like it.'

Dabiri, E. 2021
What white people can do next.
UK. Penguin Random House.
(Page 98).

Not everybody observes racist jokes as funny. Jokes hurt and damage relationships. From the target's perspective they are difficult to manage and process. They may come unexpectecly and in situations where they are least expected.

> 'Jokes can leave you feeling alone because you are the only one unable to laugh and go along with what is considered light-hearted and fun.'

Cousins, S. 2019.
Overcoming Everyday Racism.
London. Jessica Kingsley Publishers.
(Page 84).

So, once again you are excluded and may feel trapped into going along with it, just to keep safe and until you are able to leave the situation. It's important to remember that some jokes are overtly racist, and you should **reach out to friends and family for support** and in severe cases consider reporting it to the police. Some jokes are less covert and more overt; Reni-Eddo Lodge describes them as:

> 'slipping through your fingers like a water-snake toy.'

Lodge, Reni-Eddo 2017.
Why I'm no longer talking to white people about race.
London. Bloomsbury Publishing.
(Page 64).

'Most microaggressions, especially those that arise from aversive racism, contain an overt message – and the targets are often told they have misinterpreted the incident, and you are left feeling like you don't know what's really happened.'

Derald W S, Spanierman LB. 2010.
Microaggressions in Everyday Life.
NJ USA. John Wiley and Sons, Inc. (Page 99).

What to do

▶ If applicable, make a note and keep a record of who is making the joke and when and where these jokes are taking place. This information may prove useful to you if you were to make a complaint further along the line.

▶ **If the environment isn't safe, find somewhere safer and don't feel guilty about leaving an unsafe situation.**

▶ Remind yourself that it's not always your responsibility to call it out every time it happens. Saying nothing might protect you in the short term but acting once your confidence has returned is important in the long term.

▶ Alternatively, and if you feel secure, tell them that it's not okay, stand your ground and know that you are speaking the truth to a lie, the lie that this 'banter'; is acceptable when it is not.

Whatever and however you decide to manage a so-called joke, walk away with pride; it may feel like your responsibility to continue a tension filled social interaction, but you don't need to trouble yourself with its intent or subtext unless you choose to do so. **You are entitled to position yourself outside of the conversation.**

Anti-racism belongs to everyone; it is not your responsibility to educate the majority. Your social reality is made up of covert experiences, overt experiences, and everyday lived experiences of racism.

Pick your fights and choose your battles wisely, pass the battle over to someone else if you need to and be mindful of your self-care. Because anti-racist resistance requires a whole-comunity approach, the responsiblity lies with us all.

WHEN YOU ARE A **BARRISTER** AND ARE MISTAKEN FOR THE **DEFENDANT** OR THE CLEANER

Interstate Condensed Black > Baskerville > **Impact** > Arial

Being repeatedly misidentified; having to explain your role and reason for taking up your rightful place in a courtroom or any other organisation is hostile and offensive.

- It's like a stop and search for your credentials.

- It's where assumptions are made about you being seen as anything other than who you are.

- It's where you are diminished and disregarded.

- It's where the colour of your skin acts as a marker of lawlessness or wrongdoing.

- It's where you are subjected to both physical and verbal threat in your workplace.

Alexandra Wilson 'was mistaken for a defendant three times in one day at court, has called for compulsory anti-racism training at every level of the UK legal system'.
Aamna.
Sat 26th Sept 2020.
The Guardian.

Wilson described feeling exhausted and dismissed on multiple occasions. This is a system that cannot see beyond the colour of her skin; it communicates hostility, exclusion, and racism in these interpersonal reactions. These suggest a culture driven by systemic racism where black, brown professionals of colour are thrown against an environment that inflicts everyday harm.

What to do

- Wherever possible make a complaint.

"I'm not saying **YOU'RE NO GOOD AT YOUR JOB** but you're just **NOT ASSERTIVE ENOUGH.**"

Baskerville Old Face > **Interstate Compressed Black** > **Arial Black**

Some black, brown and people of colour are seen as subservient, able to be a good, kind and supportive colleagues but unable to be in command and take control. This comment is both a criticism and a put-down at the same time and it serves to keep you in your place.

It's saying 'be like us, work like us' and 'leave your cultural baggage behind', holding on to the notion that western work-related cultures are superior. Western culture persists in seeing others as all the same, but it views itself as consisting of unique individuals unfettered by a culture they simply do not see.

This is an act of stereotyping, an overgeneralisation and a form of workplace communication that is undermining and disapproving. It is a stereotype held by many and presented as the norm, reducing the target to a type of caricature removed from reality yet widely accepted even though it bears no resemblance to fact.

'The need to label, categorise and make sense of others, of different peoples, is the preoccupation of the racist, who perceives threat through contact with the other.'
Bhui, Kamaldeep (2002)
Racism and Mental Health, Prejudice and Suffering.
London. Jessica Kingsley Publishers.

When you are stereotyped, **you are seen through the lens of another who is misinformed** and holds the wrong assumptions. There are many people in the workplace who are not assertive; this is not an issue derived from skin colour; many complex factors are at work.

'Asians – both men and women – who display dominance experience more racial harassment at work than Asians who are not dominant, or other minorities who display dominance in the workplace.'
Kandola, B. (2018)
Racism at work. The danger of indifference.
Oxford. Pearn Kandola Publishing.

THE **sto**

dete

THE **sec**

AND **gua**

BEING FO

OF PURCHASE

FOR PROOF

Interstate Condensed Black > Impact > Interstate Condensed Bold

LLOWED WE

BEING QUESTIONED

re.
ctive
urity
rd

BEING ASKED

Black, brown and people of colour cannot easily hide because their visibility comes with more scrutiny and their colour identifies them as a threat, a potential shoplifter.

Being targeted by store detectives and security guards whilst going about your everyday life is a form of racial profiling: it is harassing and discriminatory.

If you are being unfairly treated in this way, followed around department stores with no justification, you are becoming an unwilling participant in a tired and outdated game that has its roots in what **Ibram X. Kendi** terms racial policy:

> **'when someone discriminates against a person in a racial group, they are carrying out a policy or taking advantage of the lack of a protective policy.'**
> Kendi, X, Ibram. 2019.
> *How to be an antiracist.*
> London. Penguin. (Page 19).

Unless you are with someone else while shopping, there is no one to protect you.

The Impact

The experience of being followed around the shops in this way is like being guarded but never being able to let your guard down. You cannot pretend you are less visible and it's exhausting: repeatedly explaining your innocence. You may end up feeling like you don't belong, feeling unwelcome in the place you live and work. You may feel in a state of constant hypervigilance: this is a feeling of enhanced sensory sensitivity that arises out of the need to constantly scan the environment for threat.

ONE
ATES
T A PERSON
IAL GROUP
E CARRYING
POLICY OR
ADVANTAGE
ACK OF A
TIVE POLICY.'

What to do

When you are feeling confident and 'up for it', you might:

▶ Explain to the shop manager that their security system is not working for you.

▶ Make a complaint: tell them that you feel you're being racially targeted and ask them what they're going to do about it and how they are going to **record the incident you're describing**.

▶ Believe in yourself and believe that you are not overreacting and that you are entitled to make a complaint and to stand up for your rights.

Today is the day to walk away, you might decide to:

▶ Make sure you always leave the store with a receipt, particularly if you check out using a machine.

▶ When buying clothes always check that security tags are removed.

▶ Find ways of calming the senses: step back and allow yourself to relax physically and emotionally.

▶ Break the circle of stress and tension, and make a conscious decision not to complain this time. Anti-racism is everyone's responsibility: you don't have to go it alone; **you don't have to accept every challenge that comes your way**. You are more than entitled to a break.

18

IF YOU DON'T SEE COLOUR THEN YOU DON'T SEE . . .

A tension-filled interaction where your skin colour is swept under the carpet and your racial and cultural heritage is denied. The intention of the speaker may well be to find common ground and position them as a good person whilst clinging to their unexamined assumption that erasing your life experiences will make you feel better about yourself.

This exchange operates at a level that ensures the deliverer:

▶ Feels good about themselves.

▶ Feels they are fair.

▶ Feels they are socially just.

▶ Is doing everything they can to build good relationships.

▶ Is showing **solidarity as a member of humanity**.

The reality is more likely to be:

▶ They don't want to walk into a conversation about race because they want to protect the status quo.

▶ **They don't want to see your race because they think they have moved beyond race**.

▶ They are suggesting that you are no different from anyone else and certainly not special.

▶ They may also be fearful of saying the wrong thing and want you to believe they had no intention to harm.

▶ This seemingly mild social interaction speaks volumes and is a poor attempt to disarm you of your life's experiences.

The Impact

▶ We ignore them.

▶ We're exhausted by them.

▶ We roll our eyes at them.

▶ **We see them coming**.

WHEN EVERYONE SITS NEXT TO EVERYONE ELSE ON THE BUS AND NOBODY SITS NEXT TO

When everyone sits next to everyone else

22

HoW CaN You aFFoRD YouR CaR?

PULL oVeR YouR CaR MuST Be SToLeN!

¡CaR! PULL IN THAT THiNG SOMe- oVeR YouR CaR MuST Be SToLeN!

You'Re HiDiNG SOMe-THiNG iN THAT CaR!

Interstate condensed Ultra Black > Bernard MT Condensed > Gotham Ultra

You are driving while innocent; suddenly you are stopped because you are 'driving while black'. You are being straightjacketed into a stereotype where your success is seen as suspicious and where there is no recognition that you have legitimate resources, earned through hard work and talent to pay for the car you happen to be driving.

This is a form of racial profiling where the colour of your skin associates you with a crime you haven't committed. The perpetrator is not reacting to any actual behaviour on your part: they are reacting to the colour of your skin.

Racial profiling is mainly carried out by the police and security guards: **it is a failure of training and is rooted in failed policy, practices and procedures.** When the target is black, brown or a person of colour, minor offences which are normally overlooked become drivers for racial abuse and harassment.

The Impact

'When police officers stopped Neomi Bennett late at night, they did not know anything about her – including that she had been awarded a British Empire Medal for services to nursing and invited to Downing Street in recognition of her work. In her opinion, they simply saw a black woman sitting in a car and asked her to get out to be searched.'

https://www.theguardian.com/world/2020/jun/18/nurse-claims-met-police-wrongfully-arrested-her-because-she-black-neomi-bennett

The bodycam footage of this event is extremely distressing: Neomi is clearly confused and frightened and yet the police persist in a threatening manner. She was arrested and later found guilty of resisting/obstructing a constable. She appealed and the Crown Prosecution Service (CPS) abandoned the case, and her conviction was thrown out.

Neomi Bennett has been diagnosed with post-traumatic stress disorder.

"You speak really good English."

"Yes, it's because i am ENGLISH!*

Big Caslon > **Impact**

*WELSH! SCOTTISH! IRISH!

The intent behind this microaggression is almost invisible as it throws us into a dialogue that is not of our making; where many assumptions lie under the statement.

Assumptions that suggest that you do not belong, that English is not your first language and that even if you were born here, you still do not belong, and you never will.

The Impact

These assumptions reinforce difference, position you as an outsider and may evoke feelings of powerlessness as you go about your life lived in the glare of whiteness.

Because the comment falls one on top of the other, it may leave you with little energy to respond effectively. You are left to assess whether the comment was intentional and, **because of repeated exposure, you will have to manage the impact on how you perceive its intentionality.** There is a history behind these words; one that is laced with patronage and condescension. The long-term impact often leaves black, brown and people of colour withdrawing from fully participating in society.

You have choices, you can challenge and confront, or as Kandola points out:

> **"Rather than managing these feelings by working unreasonably hard, or punishing ourselves with harsh self-criticism, it is better to self-soothe using kindness . . . when experiencing feelings of exclusion, otherness or inferiority."**
> Kandola, B. (2020)
> *Free to soar. Race and wellbeing in organisations.*
> Pearn Kandola Publishing.
> (Page 123)

AT THE AIR-PORT

THE SUITCASE SEARCH

The Impact

Race is a constant factor and a danger in the lives of black, brown and people of colour.

You brace yourself at the check-in desk for that extra scrutiny of your passport.

You reach security and once again you find yourself wondering "will they or won't they search your luggage?" - is the question you're asking yourself. **In general, your lived experience confirms the outcome.**

Being searched, scrutinised, and questioned at airports is a constant in the lives of black, brown and people of colour. It can be felt as either a hassle or a frightening experience. It happens so many times that it may lead to a feeling of powerlessness, loss of control over your environment and a reluctant acceptance of the status quo. **Navigating your way through hostile barriers and being a constant object of suspicion may cause anxiety, fear and distress.** It is a form of communication that once again challenges your citizenship and your sense of belonging to the country in which you live.

You find yourself in a no-win situation where taking action may be detrimental to your safety and not taking action may be detrimental to your self-worth and sense of belonging to the country you inhabit.

It's important to trust your intuition and rely on the wisdom you've gathered over many years because it will guide you and allow you to validate and acknowledge the experience as real and not something cooked up in your imagination.

28

You get to
live in a
SUBURB
and escape
to the country.

WE GET TO LIVE IN A GHETTO AND FORM A COMMUNITY.

YOU'RE NOT LIKE THE OTHERS

COPPERPLATE > **Bauhaus** > Perpetua > Goudy Old Style > **STENCIL** > Skia > **American Typewriter**

The message's undertones are clear: it's visible and yet invisible. This is a form of everyday oppression, and it often occurs when a group of friends are seemingly expressing notions of acceptance.

If you behave like 'us' and not like 'them' you will be accepted into our group. We are happy to exclude and invalidate aspects of your cultural background and you can only belong on their terms. **As long as you speak like them, live your life like them and be like them you will be included.** This involves sacrificing aspects of yourself on the altar of their culture.

The Impact

You are left to solve the problem and try to make sense of that which is not directly expressed. It's a seemingly innocent slight that will cause you maximum harm. Not only do you have to expend energy and time trying to work this out, but you will need to make a decision as to whether or not to maintain your relationships with these friends or challenge and confront the microaggression.

Either way you find yourself in a catch-22.

32

YOU TELL ME
TO GO BACK
TO A PLACE
CALLED
HOME
WITHOUT
TELLING ME
WHERE IT IS.

'The ache for home
lives in all of us,
the safe place where
we can go as we are
and not be questioned.'
Angelou, M. 2014
*Rainbow in the cloud. The Wit
and Wisdom of Maya Angelou.*
London. Virago Press.
(Page 6).

MICRO AGGRE SSIONS IN THE WORK PLACE

Small acts of exclusion that are difficult to challenge because the target can never be sure whether it was meant to be excluding.

We are often held to higher standards through invisible forms of behaviour that scale and rate us to some ill-defined norm. This can cause serious harm to black, brown and people of colour, serving to harm their motivation and connection to the workplace and to their colleagues.

We are often:
- Interrupted.
- Talked over.
- Micro-managed.
- Unrecognised.
- Overly monitored.
- Told we are being too sensitive.
- Told that it didn't really happen.
- **Undervalued and under supported in public situations**.
- Overlooked for promotion.
- Excluded from decision making processes.
- Given unequal access to professional development.
- Pressured into taking on more work.

The Impact

The target becomes acclimatised to these 'grit your teeth' moments, eventually understanding that this is just the way things are; they fall into a feeling of resignation because they cannot prove whether these interactions carry racial overtones, and they cannot find the language to fight back. **You cannot challenge what you cannot see.**

Your feeling of safety is diminished because there are no checks and balances: you remain watchful as you hold your tongue.

I'M NOT RACIST, I'VE GOT FRIENDS WHO ARE BLACK!

I'M NOT RACIST!

37

Baltica Extra Condensed > BEBAS NEUE > Interstate Condensed Ultra Black

A form of defense that is often offensive to a black, brown or person of colour.

This is a device aimed at switching off the conversation, brushing the offensive statement under the carpet, denying a different perspective and preventing a response. It's also a form of controlling and protecting oneself from holding a conversation about race; closing the dialogue and making a **claim to be innocent of the original offence**.

This is a response that's proved predictable in the lives of black, brown and people of colour.

Any suggestion that racism is at work is often met with this comment and because of its subtle message makes it almost impossible to challenge. But if black, brown and people of colour were to challenge this statement, they would have to brace themselves for yet another conversation they know they wouldn't win.

The Impact

Black, brown and people of colour collectively experience the same old responses and defences in their everyday lives; they've heard them a thousand times before and are frequently socialised into ignoring these comments because **they have been on the receiving end so many times it's become mind-numbingly tedious.** You are left to weigh up the pros and cons of taking this into an argument or responding when unhealthy forms of communication place you in a no-win situation.

WE WANT MORE EVIDENCE,

AND WE WANT MORE DATA.

Continuous requests for evidence and data won't change the story that racism is a reality.

"You're too sensitive."

Rockwell > **Interstate Condensed Ultra Black**

We are charged with being oversensitive, with 'having a chip on our shoulder'. We are placed in the wrong.

We know the times we've shut our mouths when we've sat in white spaces, and yet when we dare to speak, we are shut down yet again. Our history of staying silent is ignored. When white people call out black, brown and people of colour in such a way, they are buying into a collective response to racism because this is a form of blaming and shaming that has been used for decades.

It is an accusation, a mechanism for taking the moral high ground and a means of controlling when and where they are going to allow or put a stop to your talk about race. Not only are white people positioning themselves as experts on what it is to be sensitive, but they are seeking to close down the conversation because it is they who feel fragile and uncomfortable; not you.

The Impact

The offender has flipped the conversation to make you feel responsible, to make you feel like the culprit. Further engagement will bring further outrage and you are left to figure out how to respond. Black, brown and people of colourare:

> **"Damned if they don't (take action), and damned if they do (take action)."**
> D.W. Sue. L, Spanierman, (2020) *Microaggresssions in Everyday Life.* John Wiley & Sons, Inc. NJ. USA. (Page 79).

You are being viewed as a problem: you are in the wrong, and the cause of your own distress.

THEY ALL LOOK THE SAME TO ME

A refusal to acknowledge difference and diversity and your personal unique attributes.

You are thrown into anonymity, your individuality is of no interest, you are dismissed and are denied your singularity.

BEBAS NEUE > Google Sans > Interstate Condensed > **Arial Black** > Gotham > Frutiger > **Abadi Condensed**

THEY ALL LOOK THE SAME TO ME

A refusal to acknowledge difference and diversity and your personal unique attributes.

You are thrown into anonymity, your individuality is of no interest, you are dismissed and are denied your singularity.

HOLD ONTO YOUR

HAN

Lubalin Graph Bold

The Impact

Black, brown and people of colour are so accustomed to these interactions, they probably react unconsciously to these familiar non-verbal interactions. This is a non-verbal interaction and a form of racism that's held in the body of another person and felt and sensed by the target. It is impossible to challenge this automatic manifestation of fight, fright and flight that runs through the veins of whiteness. This is a part of our everyday experience that we shrug off as normal and yet we are trapped and excluded by this label.

Although the source of this problem is located out there and not within us, we still feel an object of intense scrutiny. In casual interactions we are reminded that we should stay in our place because our very presence makes others feel insecure, whilst the perpetrator finds themselves on the side of innocence as they go about reproducing and enacting their version of the world.

Some white people perceive danger and threat in the presence of black, brown and people of colour.

They hold a conscious or unconscious collective perception that all brown people are criminals. We are left trapped in a legacy that marks us out as dangerous and unpredictable.

"You'd get on really well with ZANE . . .

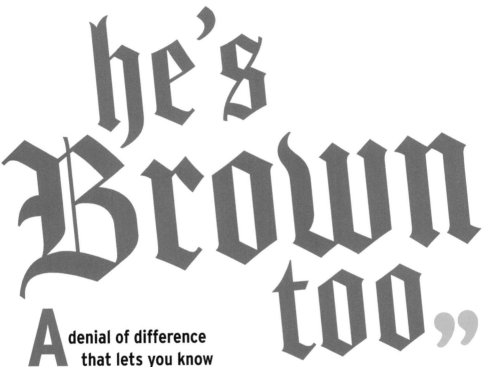

he's Brown too "

A denial of difference that lets you know you have this one thing in common, and that is the colour of your skin.

And the colour of your skin must mean you will get on well, regardless of the fact you may come from a completely different background, have different cultural beliefs, and speak a different language.

The Impact

You may have to decide whether this is a well-intentioned attempt to be inclusive or an attempt to exclude you from the dominant group because you belong 'over there' with 'them'.

48

"PEOPLE OF COLOUR JUST

DON'T APPLY FOR JOBS HERE"

A case of unexamined thinking and a flippant remark placing the fault elsewhere and outside of the organisation's policies, procedures and processes.

It might be too much effort to consider interacting with the local community in which you are based and to re-think your recruitment practices. There are no easy solutions, only hard work to undo what has been done.

The Impact

Black, brown and people of colour will not feel a sense of belonging in the workplace.

They are likely to leave; take their ideas, talent and perspectives to another place.

"

DON'T PLAY THE RACE CARD

"

‹ **is more easily understood as**

"don't EVER talk about RACE".

This form of communication is so loaded with hidden meaning that it's almost impossible to unpack.

It's a privileged attempt at devaluing anything you say about race or about your lived experience. It's also a tactic that can leave you feeling utterly powerless because you are being charged with something you haven't done. This is an accusation aimed at silencing you and setting you up to lose.

The Impact

When someone throws these words at you, **you're forcibly brought into contact with an immovable object**, an allegation that cannot bear to countenance a counter argument, however logical or however factual.

Walk away

DERAILING THE DIALOGUE

Where conversations about race are closed down, taken off the table, and where the discussion is directed away from race and racism because it challenges the status quo.

Some of the mechanisms that manoeuvre the conversation away from race are strategies that:

▶ Make the conversation about anything other than race.

▶ Focus on class instead of race - where race is positioned as an aspect of class and subordinated to class.

> **"And although working-class white and BME people have lots in common, we need to remember that although the experiences are very similar, they are also very different."**
> Eddo-Lodge, R. (2017)
> *Why I'm No Longer Talking to White People about Race.*
> London: Bloomsbury Publishing. (Page 210).

▶ Attribute racial inequality to causes other than racism.

▶ CHANGE THE SUBJECT.

▶ Focus on terminology as a means of distraction and a means of avoiding deeper and more meaningful discussions.

▶ Portray gender as the universal difference without acknowledging the failure of the feminist movement to include the lived experience of black, brown and women of colour. The feminist movement was often experienced as exclusive, both unaware of its white privilege and its manufactured alleged sense of solidarity. It unconsciously or consciously erased the lived experiences of black, brown and women of colour from its campaigns.

▶ Discuss other identities.

For us to develop a basic understanding of the impact of racism on the lives of black, brown and people of colour, we need to take space and time to **focus on race, and place it at the heart of the conversation** instead of trying to find ways that subvert and deny its existence. Race is a social construct embedded within a system that is reinforced by society, and we cannot and must not derail these conversations.

Talking about race does matter and black, brown and people of colour have something essential to contribute to this dialogue. **Our stories tell of our history - a history about which many know nothing.**

"WHY ARE YOU WEARING THAT SCARF?"

"I BET YOU'RE FORCED TO, BECAUSE OF YOUR RELIGION!"

BEBAS NEUE

Communicating hostility towards religious communities using overly probing questions is commonplace.

These questions sound harmless and yet mask a hidden meaning. Religious intolerance and prejudice are enacted in public spaces through daily interactions that reflect the tensions in our communities. Religion is both seen as a threat to the dominant culture and of no value nor useful function.

> **"We prize our own mode of existence and correspondingly underprize (or actively attack) what seems to us to threaten it."**
> Allport, W.G. (1979)
> *The Nature of Prejudice.*
> United States. Perseus Publishing.
> (Page 27).

Visible signs of religious belief, such as the hijab, may provoke unwelcome attention where black, brown and people of colour are seen as representing their entire religion and where their individual experience of religion is subsumed in the mind of another. Women wear the hijab for many different reasons, but this is often seen as a tool of oppression as opposed to a source of dignity or connection to family and social networks.

Religion provokes powerful feelings in others, generating suspicion and linking visual cues to fundamentalism, terrorism, tradition, and community.

There is often a lack of respect and understanding for religious and cultural beliefs that sit outside those of a secular society. Such beliefs are often rejected despite religion being an extremely important factor in the lives of many minority ethnic people.

The Impact

In the minds of some people, wearing a hijab operates as a symbol activating microaggressions. There is little or no understanding of the pursuit of a religious and cultural life that is enriching, celebratory and makes a positive contribution to our society. **Black, brown and people of colour are left to try and preserve their beliefs irrespective of the daily experience of microaggressions**. We need to recognise that pride in one's culture increases a sense of belonging and a sense of connection to social networks that provide a rich resource to so many.

LOOK
AFTER YOUR
WELLBEING,
SEEK
SUPPORT
AND
TAKE **CARE**
OF YOURSELF

Perpetua › *Blacksword* › Helvetica Neue Thin › **Helvetica Neue Bold**

Black, brown and people of colour have learned to live within racially-charged landscapes. Black, brown and people of colour have learned many adequate coping strategies.

Nevertheless, microaggressions whether conscious or unconscious exert psychological and physical pressure on the mind and body. This pressure is a force felt over a lifetime and it is not insignificant. Black, brown and people of colour often find themselves with a diminished sense of ease as they go about their lives braced against these daily interactions. They are left to engineer individual acts of self-protection with little guidance, recognition or support.

Microaggressions are threat-filled interactions that are emotionally burdening and may affect your wellbeing. Sometimes you will need to seek support to make sense of what is often obscured, and this emotional baggage may be hard work to resolve on your own. If you are on the receiving end of persistent and habitual microaggresive behaviour, then **seeking help from people you trust is fundamental to your wellbeing**.

The experience of microaggressions place black, brown and people of colour at greater risk of psychological damage because of prolonged and repeated negative interactions.

Your wellbeing is worth supporting, protecting and nurturing. Finding the right person to support you can be difficult, but **there are culturally competent people who recognise the existence of systemic racism and understand the impact this has on the individual**: they could be friends, family, or professionals.

"**A life filled with acceptance, appreciation, community, safety and consideration is one in which life's challenges will be more easily faced. It's advisable not to go it alone, not because you can't but because there is much to be gained from reaching out to others and staying connected to the people in your world.**"
Cousins, S. (2019)
Overcoming Everyday Racism.
London: Jessica Kingsley Publishers.
(Page 147).

Susan Cousins is the author of **Overcoming Everyday Racism: Building Resilience and Wellbeing in the Face of Discrimination and Microaggressions** (Jessica Kingsley Publishers).

Susan is Senior Compliance Advisor, Race-Religion and Belief at Cardiff University. She was the first brown counsellor to be employed by the South Avon Health Authority to work with black, brown and clients of colour in inner-city Bristol.

She has extensive experience in both counselling and supervision in the NHS and Higher Education settings. She has written for the Independent, the Psychologist, Race and Class, Psychology Today and various BACP Journals. Susan is committed and actively engaged in issues of race and its impact on psychological wellbeing.

Interstate Compressed Ultra Black

Barry Diamond took an apprenticeship route into design. He began his career briefly as a typesetter, before moving onto the drawing board and then digital design.

Barry is currently Senior Designer and Brand Manager at Cardiff University, and is involved in various side projects and collaborations. He designs **Representology: the journal of media and diversity.**

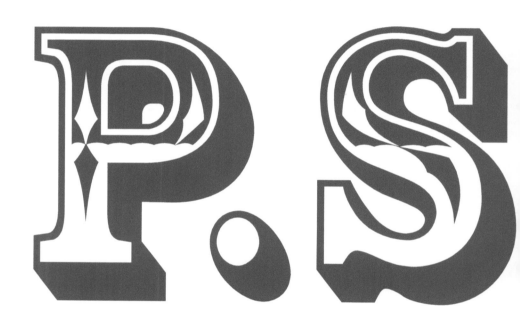

NEVER LEAVE THE SHOP WITHOUT A RECEIPT.